VIVAS TO THOSE WHO HAVE FAILED

VIVAS TO THOSE WHO HAVE FAILED

Poems

Martín Espada

W. W. NORTON & COMPANY

Independent Publishers Since 1923

NEW YORK   LONDON

For information about special discounts for bulk purchases, please contact
W. W. Norton Special Sales at specialsales@wwnorton.com or 800-233-4830

Manufacturing by Berryville Graphics
Book design by Lovedog Studio
Production manager: Julia Druskin

ISBN: 978-0-393-24903-3

W. W. Norton & Company, Inc.
500 Fifth Avenue, New York, N.Y. 10110
www.wwnorton.com

W. W. Norton & Company Ltd.
Castle House, 75/76 Wells Street, London W1T 3QT

1 2 3 4 5 6 7 8 9 0

Dedicated to the memory of my father
Francisco Luis "Frank" Espada
(1930–2014)

Contents

HERE I AM

A MILLION ANTS SWARMING THROUGH HIS BODY

EL MORIVIVÍ

Acknowledgments

These poems have appeared or will appear in the following publications, to whose editors grateful acknowledgment is made:

Aethelon: "The Socialist in the Crowd"

The American Poetry Review: "The Discovery of Archaeopteryx," "The Goddamned Crucifix," "Here I Am," "The Sinking of the *San Jacinto*," "Vivas to Those Who Have Failed: The Paterson Silk Strike, 1913"

Anthology of Modern American Poetry (Oxford University Press): "The Right Foot of Juan de Oñate," "Hard-Handed Men of Athens"

Cutthroat: "Haunt Me"

Drunken Boat (online): "The Right Foot of Juan de Oñate"

Goodbye, México: *Poems of Remembrance* (Texas Review Press): "The Right Foot of Juan de Oñate"

The Great Falls: *Poems About Paterson, New Jersey*: "Vivas to Those Who Have Failed: The Paterson Silk Strike, 1913"

The Great Sympathetic: Walt Whitman and the North American Review (North American Review Press): "Barbaric Yawp Big Noise Blues," "How We Could Have Lived or Died This Way"

Hanging Loose: "Flowers and Bullets," "From the *Rubáiyát of Fenway Park*," "The Right Foot of Juan de Oñate"

Harvard Review: "The Shamrock"

Irish Examiner: "The Shamrock"

La Bloga (online): "El Morivivi"

Michigan Quarterly Review: "A Million Ants Swarming Through His Body," "Marshmallow Rice Krispie Treat Machu Picchu"

Milk: "The Right Foot of Juan de Oñate"

Morning Star: "The Socialist in the Crowd," "How We Could Have Lived or Died This Way"

Naked Punch: "Haunt Me," "The Beating Heart of the Wristwatch," "The Right Foot of Juan de Oñate," "How We Could Have Lived or Died This Way," "A Million Ants Swarming Through His Body"

Nautilus II: "Ghazal for a Tall Boy from New Hampshire"

North American Review: "Heal the Cracks in the Bell of the World," "Mad Love," "Barbaric Yawp Big Noise Blues"

The Norton Introduction to Literature (W. W. Norton): "Of the Threads That Connect the Stars"

Paterson Literary Review: "After the God That Rose Like the God of Geese," "Bills to Pay," "Once Thundering Penguin Herds Darkened the Prairie," "Chalkboard on the Wall of a Diner in Providence, Rhode Island the Morning After George Zimmerman Was Acquitted in the Shooting Death of Trayvon Martin, an Unarmed Black Teenager"

Ploughshares: "Of the Threads That Connect the Stars"

Poetry Salzburg Review: "Mad Love," "Bills to Pay," "The Shamrock"

Policing the Planet (Verso): "How We Could Have Lived or Died This Way"

Post Road: "There But Not There"

Prairie Schooner: "El Morivivi," "On the Hovering of Souls and Balloon Animals," "Hard-Handed Men of Athens"

The Progressive: "Castles for the Laborers and Ballgames on the Radio," "The Beating Heart of the Wristwatch"

Saudades: Poems by José "Joe" Gouveia (Casa Mariposa Press): "Here I Am"

The Stinging Fly: "The Man in the Duck Suit"

Stonecoast Review: "Castles for the Laborers and Ballgames on the Radio," "The Right Foot of Juan de Oñate," "Heal the Cracks in the Bell of the World"

Many thanks to the community of poets that supported and inspired this work: Jack Agüeros, Doug Anderson, Chris Brandt, Sarah Browning, Sandra Cisneros, Patrick Cotter, Kwame Dawes, Chard deNiord, Maria Mazziotti Gillan, Joe Gouveia, Sam Hamill, Major Jackson, Paul Mariani, Rich Michelson, John Murillo, Marilyn Nelson, Alicia Ostriker, Oscar Sarmiento, Lauren Schmidt, Julia Shipley, Gary Soto, Rich Villar and Afaa Weaver.

Many thanks also to the Poetry Society of America for the 2013 Shelley Memorial Award, and to Andy Shallal for the 2014 Busboys and Poets Award.

VIVAS

TO THOSE

WHO HAVE

FAILED

VIVAS TO THOSE WHO HAVE FAILED:
THE PATERSON SILK STRIKE, 1913

Vivas to those who have fail'd!
And to those whose war-vessels sank in the sea!
And to those themselves who sank in the sea!
And to all generals that lost engagements, and all overcome heroes!
And the numberless unknown heroes equal to the greatest heroes known!

—*Walt Whitman*

I. The Red Flag

The newspapers said the strikers would hoist
the red flag of anarchy over the silk mills
of Paterson. At the strike meeting, a dyers' helper
from Naples rose as if from the steam of his labor,
lifted up his hand and said *Here is the red flag*:
brightly stained with dye for the silk of bow ties
and scarves, the skin and fingernails boiled away
for six dollars a week in the dye house.

He sat down without another word, sank back
into the fumes, name and face rubbed off
by oblivion's thumb like a Roman coin
from the earth of his birthplace dug up
after a thousand years, as the strikers
shouted the only praise he would ever hear.

II. The River Floods the Avenue

He was the other Valentino, not the romantic sheik
and bullfighter of silent movie palaces who died too young,
but the Valentino standing on his stoop to watch detectives
hired by the company bully strikebreakers onto a trolley
and a chorus of strikers bellowing the banned word *scab*.
He was not a striker or a scab, but the bullet fired to scatter
the crowd pulled the cork in the wine barrel of Valentino's back.
His body, pale as the wings of a moth, lay beside his big-bellied wife.

Two white-veiled horses pulled the carriage to the cemetery.
Twenty thousand strikers walked behind the hearse, flooding
the avenue like the river that lit up the mills, surging around
the tombstones. *Blood for blood*, cried Tresca: at his signal,
thousands of hands dropped red carnations and ribbons
into the grave, till the coffin evaporated in a red sea.

III. The Insects in the Soup

Reed was a Harvard man. He wrote for the New York magazines.
Big Bill, the organizer, fixed his one good eye on Reed and told him
of the strike. He stood on a tenement porch across from the mill
to escape the rain and listen to the weavers. The bluecoats
told him to move on. The Harvard man asked for a name to go
with the number on the badge, and the cops tried to unscrew
his arms from their sockets. When the judge asked his business,
Reed said: *Poet.* The judge said: *Twenty days in the county jail.*

Reed was a Harvard man. He taught the strikers Harvard songs,
the tunes to sing with rebel words at the gates of the mill. The strikers
taught him how to spot the insects in the soup, speaking in tongues
the gospel of One Big Union and the eight-hour day, cramming the jail
till the weary jailers had to unlock the doors. Reed would write:
There's war in Paterson. After it was over, he rode with Pancho Villa.

IV. The Little Agitator

The cops on horseback charged into the picket line.
The weavers raised their hands across their faces,
hands that knew the loom as their fathers' hands
knew the loom, and the billy clubs broke their fingers.
Hannah was seventeen, the captain of the picket line,
the Joan of Arc of the Silk Strike. The prosecutor called her
a little agitator. Shame, said the judge; if she picketed again,
he would ship her to the State Home for Girls in Trenton.

Hannah left the courthouse to picket the mill. She chased
a strikebreaker down the street, yelling in Yiddish the word
for shame. Back in court, she hissed at the judge's sentence
of another striker. Hannah got twenty days in jail for hissing.
She sang all the way to jail. After the strike came the blacklist,
the counter at her husband's candy store, the words for shame.

V. Vivas to Those Who Have Failed

Strikers without shoes lose strikes. Twenty years after the weavers
and dyers' helpers returned hollow-eyed to the loom and the steam,
Mazziotti led the other silk mill workers marching down the avenue
in Paterson, singing the old union songs for five cents more an hour.
Once again, the nightsticks cracked cheekbones like teacups.
Mazziotti pressed both hands to his head, squeezing red ribbons
from his scalp. There would be no Buffalo nickel for an hour's work
at the mill, for the silk of bow ties and scarves. Skull remembered wood.

The brain thrown against the wall of the skull remembered too:
the Sons of Italy, the Workmen's Circle, Local 152, Industrial
Workers of the World, one-eyed Big Bill and Flynn the Rebel Girl
speaking in tongues to thousands the prophecy of an eight-hour day.
Mazziotti's son would become a doctor, his daughter a poet.
Vivas to those who have failed: for they become the river.

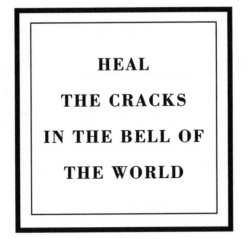

HEAL
THE CRACKS
IN THE BELL OF
THE WORLD

THE RIGHT FOOT OF JUAN DE OÑATE

for John Nichols and Arturo Madrid

On the road to Taos, in the town of Alcalde, the bronze statue
of Juan de Oñate, the conquistador, kept vigil from his horse.
Late one night a chainsaw sliced off his right foot, stuttering
through the ball of his ankle, as Oñate's spirit scratched
and howled like a dog trapped within the bronze body.

Four centuries ago, after his cannon fire burst to burn hundreds
of bodies and blacken the adobe walls of the Acoma Pueblo,
Oñate wheeled on his startled horse and spoke the decree:
all Acoma males above the age of twenty-five would be punished
by amputation of the right foot. Spanish knives sawed through ankles;
Spanish hands tossed feet into piles like fish at the marketplace.
There was prayer and wailing in a language Oñate did not speak.

Now, at the airport in El Paso, across the river from Juárez,
another bronze statue of Oñate rises on a horse frozen in fury.
The city fathers smash champagne bottles across the horse's legs
to christen the statue, and Oñate's spirit remembers the chainsaw
carving through the ball of his ankle. The Acoma Pueblo still stands.
Thousands of brown feet walk across the border, the desert
of Chihuahua, the shallow places of the Río Grande, the bridges

from Juárez to El Paso. Oñate keeps watch, high on horseback
above the Río Grande, the law of the conquistador rolled
in his hand, helpless as a man with an amputated foot,
spirit scratching and howling like a dog within the bronze body.

HEAL THE CRACKS IN THE BELL OF THE WORLD

*for the community of Newtown, Connecticut, where
twenty students and six educators lost their lives to a gunman
at Sandy Hook Elementary School, December 14, 2012*

Now the bells speak with their tongues of bronze.
Now the bells open their mouths of bronze to say:
Listen to the bells a world away. Listen to the bell in the ruins
of a city where children gathered copper shells like beach glass,
and the copper boiled in the foundry, and the bell born
in the foundry says: *I was born of bullets, but now I sing
of a world where bullets melt into bells.* Listen to the bell
in a city where cannons from the armies of the Great War
sank into molten metal bubbling like a vat of chocolate,
and the many mouths that once spoke the tongue of smoke
form the one mouth of a bell that says: *I was born of cannons,
but now I sing of a world where cannons melt into bells.*

Listen to the bells in a town with a flagpole on Main Street,
a rooster weathervane keeping watch atop the Meeting House,
the congregation gathering to sing in times of great silence.
Here the bells rock their heads of bronze as if to say:
Melt the bullets into bells, melt the bullets into bells.
Here the bells raise their heavy heads as if to say:
Melt the cannons into bells, melt the cannons into bells.

Here the bells sing of a world where weapons crumble deep
in the earth, and no one remembers where they were buried.
Now the bells pass the word at midnight in the ancient language
of bronze, from bell to bell, like ships smuggling news of liberation
from island to island, the song rippling through the clouds.

Now the bells chime like the muscle beating in every chest,
heal the cracks in the bell of every face listening to the bells.
The chimes heal the cracks in the bell of the moon.
The chimes heal the cracks in the bell of the world.

HOW WE COULD HAVE LIVED OR DIED THIS WAY

Not songs of loyalty alone are these,

But songs of insurrection also,

For I am the sworn poet of every dauntless rebel the world over.

—Walt Whitman

I see the dark-skinned bodies falling in the street as their ancestors fell

before the whip and steel, the last blood pooling, the last breath spitting.

I see the immigrant street vendor flashing his wallet to the cops,

shot so many times there are bullet holes in the soles of his feet.

I see the deaf woodcarver and his pocketknife, crossing the street

in front of a cop who yells, then fires. I see the drug raid, the wrong

door kicked in, the minister's heart seizing up. I see the man hawking

a fistful of cigarettes, the cop's chokehold that makes his wheezing

lungs stop wheezing forever. I am in the crowd, at the window,

kneeling beside the body left on the asphalt for hours, covered in a sheet.

I see the suicides: the conga player handcuffed for drumming on the subway,

hanged in the jail cell with his hands cuffed behind him; the suspect leaking

blood from his chest in the backseat of the squad car; the 300-pound boy

said to stampede bare-handed into the bullets drilling his forehead.

I see the coroner nodding, the words he types in his report burrowing

into the skin like more bullets. I see the government investigations stacking,

words buzzing on the page, then suffocated as bees suffocate in a jar. I see
the next Black man, fleeing as the fugitive slave once fled the slave-catcher,
shot in the back for a broken tail-light. I see the cop handcuff the corpse.

I see the rebels marching, hands upraised before the riot squads,
faces in bandannas against the tear gas, and I walk beside them unseen.
I see the poets, who will write the songs of insurrection generations unborn
will read or hear a century from now, words that make them wonder
how we could have lived or died this way, how the descendants of slaves
still fled and the descendants of slave-catchers still shot them, how we awoke
every morning without the blood of the dead sweating from every pore.

CHALKBOARD ON THE WALL OF A DINER IN PROVIDENCE, RHODE ISLAND THE MORNING AFTER GEORGE ZIMMERMAN WAS ACQUITTED IN THE SHOOTING DEATH OF TRAYVON MARTIN, AN UNARMED BLACK TEENAGER

Injustice anywhere is a threat to justice everywhere—MLK

Daily Special: vegetarian chili

GHAZAL FOR A TALL BOY FROM NEW HAMPSHIRE

*for Jim Foley, journalist beheaded on video by ISIS (Islamic
State of Iraq and al-Sham), August 19, 2014*

The reporters called and asked me: *Did you know him?*
I was his teacher, I said many times that day. *Yes, I knew him.*

Once he was a teacher too, teaching in another mill town
where the mills have disappeared. There, they knew him.

He taught the refugees from an island where the landlords
left them nothing but their hands. In Spanish, they knew him.

They sounded out the English, made the crippled letters
walk across the page for him, all because they knew him.

He ate their rice and beans, held their infants, posed with them
for snapshots at the graduation. Ask them how they knew him.

Beliza, Mónica, Limary: with him they wrote a poem of waterfalls
and frogs that sing at night, so he could know them as they knew him.

We know his words turn to rain in the rain forest of the poem.
We cannot say what words are his, even though we knew him.

His face on the front page sold the newspapers in the checkout line.
His executioners and his president spoke of him as if they knew him.

The reporter with the camera asked me if I saw the video his killers
wanted us to see. I muttered through a cage of teeth: *No. I knew him.*

Once he was a tall boy from New Hampshire, standing in my doorway.
He spoke Spanish. He wanted to teach. I knew him. I never knew him.

HERE I AM

HERE I AM

for José "JoeGo" Gouveia (1964–2014)

He swaggered into the room, a poet at a gathering of poets,
and the drinkers stopped crowding the cash bar, the talkers stopped
their tongues, the music stopped hammering the walls, the way
a saloon falls silent when a gunslinger knocks open the swinging doors:
JoeGo grinning in gray stubble and wraparound shades, leather Harley
vest, shirt yellow as a prospector's hallucination, sleeve buttoned
to hide the bandage on his arm where the IV pumped chemo through
his body a few hours ago. The nurse swabbed the puncture and told him
he could go, and JoeGo would go, gunning his red van from the Cape
to Boston, striding past the cops who guarded the hallways of the grand
convention center, as if to say *Here I am*: the butcher's son, the Portagee,
the roofer, the carpenter, the cabdriver, the biker-poet. This was JoeGo,
who would shout his ode to Evel Knievel in biker bars till the brawlers
rolled in beer and broken glass, who married Josy from Brazil
on the beach after the oncologist told him he had two months to live
two years ago. *That's not enough for me*, he said, and will say again
when the cancer comes back to coil around his belly and squeeze hard
like a python set free and starving in the swamp. He calls me on his cell
from the hospital, and I can hear him scream when they press the cold
X-ray plates to his belly, but he will not drop the phone. He wants
the surgery today, right now, surrounded by doctors with hands
blood-speckled like the hands of his father the butcher, sawing

through the meat for the family feast. The patient's chart should read:
This is JoeGo: after every crucifixion, he snaps the cross across his back
for firewood. He will roll the stone from the mouth of his tomb and bowl
a strike. On the night he silenced the drinkers chewing ice in my ear,
a voice in my ear said: *What the hell is that man doing here?*
And I said: *That man there? That man will live forever.*

BARBARIC YAWP BIG NOISE BLUES

for David Lenson

The Professor played saxophone for the Reprobate Blues Band,
rocking the horn like an unrepentant sinner at the poet's wedding.
I was the best man, and the band howled at my punch lines about
the president while the bride's family made Republican faces at me.
Later, in the dark, The Professor passed a joint to the harp player,
remembering a thousand gigs in the firefly-light of the reefer,
a night of saxophone delirium with John Lee Hooker, who broke
a string on his guitar and chanted *Boogie with the Hook.*

That was before the poet caught his wife at Foxwoods Casino
gambling away the rent money. That was before the harp player
hanged himself from the tree in his front yard. That was before
the stroke blacked out the luminous city in The Professor's brain.

I tracked him down at the nursing home on a hill hidden from the town.
He labored to drop the jigsaw puzzle pieces of words into the empty
spaces. The label on the door said *door;* the label on the bed said *bed;*
the label on the window said *window.* The saxophone was a brass
question mark leaning in the corner, blues improvisation banned
by the nurses to keep the patients drowsing in sedation and soup.
The man with the white beard two doors down was born in 1819,
said The Professor. *You mean 1918,* I said, unscrambling the code.

I escorted him to the picnic table in the middle of the parking lot,
slipping Whitman's *Leaves* from my back pocket like contraband.
The Professor saw the face on the cover, and the words cranked
the wheels of his jaw: *I. Celebrate. Myself.* Blues improvisation
broke out in the parking lot. I would read and he would riff:
Yes. Right. Fantastic. I read: *I am the man, I suffer'd, I was there.*
The Professor whispered: *How does he know?* as if the bearded
seer in the poems could see him sitting at the picnic table.
I read: *I sound my barbaric yawp over the roofs of the world.*
The Professor heard a band so loud the neighbors called the cops.
That's what I need, he said. *I can't make that big noise for myself.*

I left The Professor at the nursing home on the hill. I left Whitman too.
Tonight, the label on the door says *yawp*. The label on the bed says *yawp*.
The label on the window says *yawp*. The Professor swings on his saxophone
in the parking lot, oblivious to the security guards who rush to tackle him,
horn honking like a great arrowhead of geese in the sky: *Yawp. Yawp. Yawp.*

ONCE THUNDERING PENGUIN HERDS DARKENED THE PRAIRIE

I. Poetry for Tourists

The poets bring poetry to the Coney Island Aquarium,
around the corner from the wooden rollercoaster
creaking since 1927, tourists staggering away queasy,
yet hungry for a hot dog on the boardwalk. We will
tempt them to taste the steamed tofu dog of poetry instead.

II. Poetry for Jellyfish

Tonight, we declaim poems at the jellyfish exhibit,
creatures that plummet like parachutes of light,
illuminated mushrooms zooming sideways, amusing
themselves, oblivious to the nuances of alliteration
and assonance, silently refusing to clap after the last poem.

III. Poetry for Penguins

The voice of a poet on a loop, installed in the penguin
exhibit, booms out poetry in praise of penguins:
Once thundering penguin herds darkened the prairie.
Once flocks of flapping penguins blocked out the sun.

Now they cower behind a rock, peeking, ducking down,
listening to poetry for penguins, hearing only the rumble
of the Almighty Orca opening his jaws on Judgment Day.

IV. No Poetry for the Octopus or the Security Guard

The Coney Island Aquarium is closed. We are locked in.
The octopus glares at us with one huge eye. No one fed
him today. No one read him any poems. We panic and flap
like flightless birds. We rattle the gate, wailing in chorus:
We are the poets. Let us out. The security guard glares
at us with one huge eye. No one fed him today. No one
read him any poems. He unlocks the gate anyway.

CASTLES FOR THE LABORERS AND BALLGAMES ON THE RADIO

for Howard Zinn (1922–2010)

We stood together at the top of his icy steps, without a word for once,
squinting at the hill below and the tumble we were about to take,
heads bumping on every step till our bodies rolled into the street.
He was older than the breadlines of the Great Depression. Before the War,
he labored at the Brooklyn Navy Yard, even organized apprentices, but now
there was ice. I outweighed him by a hundred pounds; when my feet began
to skid, I would land on him and hear the crunch of his surgically repaired spine.
The books I held for him would fly away like doves disobeying an amateur magician.

Let's go back in the house, I said. *Show me the baseball Sandy Koufax signed to you:
"From one lefty to another."* Instead, he picked up a blue plastic bucket of sand,
the kind of pail good for building castles at Coney Island, tossed a fist of sand
down onto the sun-frozen concrete and took the first step, delicately. Again
and again, he would throw a handful of sand in the air like bread for pigeons,
then probe with the tip of his shoe for the sandy place on the next step:
sand, then step; sand, then step. Every time he took a step I took a step,
an apprentice shadow studying the movements of his teacher the body.
This is how I came to dance a soft-shoe in size fourteen boots, grinding
my toes into the gritty spots he left behind on the ice. I was there:

I saw him turn the tundra into the beach with a wave of his hand,

Coney Island of castles for the laborers and ballgames on the radio,

showing the way across the ice and down the hill into the street,

where he spoke to me the last words of the last lesson: *You drive.*

THE SOCIALIST IN THE CROWD

Fenway Park, Boston, May 2013

A baseball sailing into the crowd makes monsters of us all.
Hands claw the air as if to snatch a trophy of war,
the enemy's white skull to dangle at the gates of the city
as a warning to others. Big-bellied men chase the prey
down the steps of the bleachers, hearts grinding like millstones.
Drunks tumble onto the field along the third base line.
The ball stings, fractures fingers, yet we stretch hands to heaven,
groping for a foul pop stuffed with the winning lottery number,
a line drive scorched with the face of Jesus on cowhide.
We are ravenous for the flesh of a baseball, mouths open
to tear the stitches and bite into the tough, white fruit.
We slap the ball away from the catcher's mitt, the left fielder's leap.
There are fistfights. There are lawsuits. There are baseballs
that escape in the tangle of bodies, skipping back onto the field.

This afternoon, the ball ricochets off the woman with a beer
in one fist and a hard lemonade in the other, then the man stuck
in his popcorn box like a bear with a paw jammed in the honey jar,
hopping into the hands of the socialist in my row. She hands
the ball to a boy wearing the uniform of the Red Sox, cap too big
for his head, and he gazes at the red stitches the way he once studied
the first caterpillar on his fingertips. I have never caught a ball
in the stands, at Fenway or the Polo Grounds or that ballpark in Havana.

Bad socialist that I am, I would have kept it. The crowd would jeer
the socialist who did not stand for the anthem or another sergeant
singing *God Bless America* in the seventh inning. Yet, within the monster
of the crowd grinds the gristmill heart of a socialist, so they clap
and whoop when she hands the ball to the boy, then gasp at the *boom*
of the right fielder's body slamming off the wall, waiting for the next ball
to come their way, like the winning lottery number or the face of Jesus.

FROM THE *RUBÁIYÁT OF FENWAY PARK*

The hanging curveball hangs, and having hung,
Is hit: nor pitcher with his cursing tongue
Shall lure it back from deep in bleacher seats,
Nor all his tears from dugout towel wrung.

HARD-HANDED MEN OF ATHENS

Theseus: What are they that do play it?

Philostrate: Hard-handed men, that work in Athens here,

Which never labour'd in their minds till now.

—A Midsummer Night's Dream, Act V, Scene i

We are the hard-handed men of Athens, the rude Mechanicals:
the tailor, the weaver, the tinker, the bellows-mender.
Tonight, we are actors in the forest, off the grid, surrounded
in the dark by fairies and spirits, snakes and coyotes.
Carnivorous vegans live in these woods. They leave the drum circle
to nibble at the sliced ham I smuggle in the folds of my costume.

I am three hundred pounds. The director of the company
saw me and said: *You are the Wall.* Two weeks ago, I fell
off a wall, stepping into the darkness like a cartoon character
walking on air, waving *bye-bye.* I belly-flopped in a puddle of mud.
An elderly bystander, as if on cue, spoke her only line: *Are you OK?*
I am not OK. I have a fractured elbow. I wear a sling under my Wall costume,
the Styrofoam bricks and plastic vines, the wooden beam across my shoulders.
I cannot remember my lines. I hide the script in my sling with the ham.

The play begins. No one can find Lysander. He is in the bathroom
with dysentery. Theseus improvises dialogue in iambic pentameter.
His voice echoes and scares the coyotes in the hills. They howl
back at him. A snake writes his name in the dirt by my feet.

I tell no one. I don't want the fairies to panic. Cobweb and Mustardseed
might run into the tiki torches, and then their fairy wings would explode,
and the nearest hospital is forty miles away. The tiki torches
are the only source of light off the grid. It's Shakespeare in the Dark.
The woman playing Peter Quince is mean to small children.
When Bottom turns into a donkey and the Mechanicals flee,
I stand behind her and let her bounce off my chest. She falls down.
I want her to fall down. I ask: *Are you OK?* She is not OK. Fairy Queen
Titania's bed sways in the trees, threatening to topple and kill us all.

At the wedding of Theseus, Duke of Athens, we play Pyramus and Thisbe.
The aristocrats laugh at us, real actors on loan from the highbrow
Shakespearean company in the valley, and we snarl back at them.
I am the Wall. I am inspired. I lift Pyramus and Thisbe into the air
and slam them together for their kiss. The beam across my shoulders
cracks. The crack alarms the carnivorous vegans on picnic blankets
watching the show. Some think the crack is my leg breaking. Some think
the crack is a gunshot. Suddenly, it's Ford's Theatre and I'm Lincoln.
Or maybe I'm John Wilkes Booth. The jagged beam presses into my neck,
against the artery in my neck, like the fangs of a vampire hungry for ham. `
One stumble and *A Midsummer Night's Dream* ends in a bloodbath.

I bellow my last line: *Thus Wall away doth go.* I do a soft-shoe offstage.
Five people pull the Wall costume over my head. Somebody asks: *Are you OK?*
I am not OK. Then, I see my son onstage. He is twelve. He is Moonshine.
He cradles a half-blind Chihuahua and says: *This dog, my dog.*
He lifts his lantern high, and his lantern is the moon. Even the sneering
Hippolyta, Queen of the Amazons, must admit: *Well shone, Moon.*

This moon shines like an uncirculated Kennedy half-dollar from the days when Kennedy was a martyred saint. The coyotes do not howl. The crickets fall silent. Even the fairies cease their gossip and giggling. We are the hard-handed men of Athens. This dog is our dog.

MARSHMALLOW RICE KRISPIE TREAT
MACHU PICCHU

We stormed the abandoned railroad station in the city to play
As You Like It set in the Summer of Love. We wore bell-bottoms
and painted our faces. We entered to Hendrix and *Purple Haze*,
tossing roses to the lovers on picnic blankets. We yelled the words
of the Bard over the pandemonium of freight trains, the blues festival
thumping down the street, the demolition derby. *All the world's a stage*,
cried melancholy Jaques, more melancholy still when loudspeakers
ecstatic at the crash of cars drowned out The Seven Ages of Man.
We leapt in hippie costume off the stage to chase the teetering drunks
away from the baby carriages in the crowd. We spied on the crowd
behind the curtain, and somebody said: *Why aren't they laughing?*

I was Charles the wrestler. I would wheeze my lines like a man punched
in the throat, a tribute to Anthony Quinn in *Requiem for a Heavyweight*.
I wore a rhinestone belt across my belly that said *Champ*, dragging
my leg in a brace offstage to kick down a stack of aluminum trash cans,
the clamor of their collapse simulating defeat in the match with Orlando,
the hero strutting through the play, who couldn't puzzle out that clever
Rosalind was a girl dressed as a boy, teaching him how to woo her.
My son was Touchstone the clown, smacking Corin the shepherd
with a rubber chicken till the vegans protested the abuse of the chicken,
flinging a dozen rubber snakes in the face of William the country boy
till the vegans protested the abuse of snakes, squirting a plastic flower
at everyone and offending no one, since the flower would backfire

and the water would darken his pants. The director's half-blind dog
barked whenever Silvius the shepherd chased the spitting Phebe
through the lovers on blankets, the baby carriages and the drunks,
who cheered the loudest till we drove them from the Forest of Arden.

Today is my fiftieth birthday. The company storms my house to celebrate
like the brawling Shakespeareans they have seen in movies. On the way,
they stop to raid the liquor store, pirates plundering a merchant ship
to carry off every last bottle, singing pirate songs. Enter Touchstone
the clown, melancholy Jaques, William the country boy, Orlando
the hero, clever Rosalind, Corin and Sylvius the shepherds, Phebe
spitting at everyone even out of character, and Phebe's mother,
wheeling her creation through the door: Marshmallow Rice Krispie
Treat Machu Picchu. I anticipated a pound cake with one candle,
not this homage to Neruda and his epic, this place of pilgrimage
high in the Andes served up as a blasphemous and crunchy snack.
Centuries ago, laborers raised tons of stone without the wheel
to build Machu Picchu; Pizarro and his army of conquistadores
missed it, leaving the stones untouched. Now, hands snap off towers,
crack walls, wreck temples, stuffing sticky rubble into mouths.
Marshmallow Rice Krispie Treat Machu Picchu lies in ruins.

The sugar is the ember of a cigarette flicked into the combustible sewage
of beer, wine and rum. Soon, William is on all fours in the bathroom,
emptying his belly inches from the toilet, pink foam bubbling
on his lips like *the bubble reputation even in the cannon's mouth*;
Sylvius staggers across the living room to escape Phebe, banging
into a bookcase, scattering the balsawood egrets of Nicaragua

at his feet; Corin clutches a pillow in the bedroom, eyes like the eyes
of a praying mantis, left alone by Rosalind to watch a DVD of *The Crucible*,
moaning: *How does it end? They can't do this! They can't hang these people!*

At 5 AM, the director rises in the kitchen to announce that she
will fly everyone to Paris, and the grand gesture of her arm
sweeps Touchstone's sushi plate to the floor, smashing it to shards.
Actors dangle from couches and chairs. They may not be breathing.
A stranger with a Great Dane forages through bottles in the backyard.
The beast whines and sniffs the air; the Forest of Arden is burning.

I am fifty years old. I am hiding. I lock myself in the room where
I write, surrounded by the smoke-damaged books of poets long
gone to oblivion, *sans teeth, sans eyes, sans taste, sans everything.*

THE MAN IN THE DUCK SUIT

for Todd Godwin (1957–2011)

He wore a duck suit for my Super 8 movie,
back in the days when I wanted to make movies,
before I found out that I couldn't buy
cameras or film with food stamps. I borrowed
a camera and a shotgun, then rented a duck costume
for the star of my crime thriller, *In Cold Duck.*

In between takes, he would pull the duck's head off
and tuck it underneath his arm, half-human, half-waterfowl,
curly beard and bright yellow feathers, a creature from the mythology
of ancient Assyria pontificating in a New Jersey British accent
about the art of improvisation. After the last take,
he wandered out onto my porch in full duck regalia,
waving the shotgun at passing cars on Johnson Street.

Thirty years later, the hunters of Wisconsin still shiver in the reeds
as they recall the Monster Duck who hunted humans. I know
he was only a man in a duck suit, a secret I can now reveal.
He was my Bigfoot, glimpsed on grainy film, the camera shaking.

A MILLION
ANTS SWARMING
THROUGH
HIS BODY

FLOWERS AND BULLETS

Cuba and Puerto Rico
are two wings of the same bird:
they receive flowers and bullets
in the same heart.

—*Lola Rodríguez de Tió, 1889*

Tattoo the Puerto Rican flag on my shoulder.
Stain the skin red, white and blue, not the colors
that snap over holiday parades or sag over the graves
of veterans in the States, but the colors of Cuba reversed:
a flag for the rebels in the hills of Puerto Rico, dreamt up
by Puerto Rican exiles in the Cuban Revolutionary Party,
bearded and bespectacled in the sleet of New York,
Wise Men lost on their way to Bethlehem. That
was 1895, the same year José Martí would die,
poet shot from a white horse in his first battle.

Tattoo the Puerto Rican flag on my shoulder,
so if I close my eyes forever in the cold
and the doctors cannot tell the cause of death,
you will know that I died like José Martí,
with flowers and bullets in my heart.

A MILLION ANTS SWARMING THROUGH HIS BODY

for José "Chegüí" Torres (1936–2009)

There is no storyteller like a storyteller with a broken nose.
Chegüí would jab my chest before he told the tale, and I would listen.
He was Puerto Rican, like me, and used to be the champion of the world.

He learned his English at the Army base in Baltimore, cracking
the sergeant's ribs and jaw with a double left hook, body and head,
after the Black boys in the barracks taught him what the sergeant
meant by saying: *Get up nigger. Get up spic.* Years later,
the sergeant would ask, *Do you remember me?* and thank him.

The same left hook knifed the liver of Willie Pastrano at the Garden,
and he sank to the ropes, a million ants swarming through his body.
Three rounds later, the referee would tell him: *You have nothing left.*
The Puerto Ricans at the Garden sang and punched the air for Chegüí
de Playa Ponce, el campeón, a savior without nails hammered in his hands.

The next day, Chegüí awoke with swollen knuckles. He spoke
from a fire escape at Lexington and 110th Street in El Barrio
to the Puerto Ricans who gathered in the thousands, roaring
at every word, janitors and dishwashers ready to march
and burn down the mayor's mansion at his command.
I won the title for all of us, he shouted, and the fire escape
shuddered beneath his feet, demon rust loosening the bolts.

One night at the Garden he would fall, legs gone, a million ants
swarming through his body. When he fell, two men in the crowd
had heart attacks and one of them died. Chegüí would somehow
rise and swing, leave Devil Green facedown on the canvas, stumble
to his corner and tell himself: *You have nothing left.* He used to be
the champion of the world; now, he was a storyteller with a broken nose.

There is no storyteller like a storyteller with a broken nose, but even
he was not immune to diabetes, the Puerto Rican plague merciless
as rust. The scaffold of the fire escape would drop beneath him,
champion of the world and Spanish Harlem, savior of the janitors,
dishwashers and poets, as it does for all champions and saviors,
as it does for all of us in the happy crowd, singing and punching the air.

THE DISCOVERY OF ARCHAEOPTERYX

My grandfather's hands raised the rooster up for all the boys to see.
I was a Brooklyn boy lost in the Puerto Rico of my grandfather,
carsick from backseat journeys through the mountains that dipped
and rolled like a green serpent undulating through the sea.

I had never seen a rooster. Once, I saw a cow in a pen at Beachcomber Bill's
in Coney Island, and climbed the rail to stroke the huge head between
the eyes. My shirttails hung out and the cow began to chew the cloth.
The cow kept chewing till my father yanked me by the arm.

At last, Puerto Rico stopped dipping and rolling through the sea.
Here was Archaeopteryx, the feathered reptile, the dinosaur bird,
the fossil made flesh, risen screeching from the rock. I was dumbstruck
by the blackness of the tail, the beak and spurs that kept my fingers away.

My grandfather's hands calmed the ticking of the rooster's heart, the same
brown hands that beckoned me with blessings in Spanish at Christmas.
My first word was *hat*, and my grandfather's straw fedora was the first hat,
the same hat shading his eyes the day he showed me the first rooster.

As a boy, my father learned about roosters. He saw my grandfather
guide the bird into the pit, the wagers change hands, the gallos de pelea
whirl and slash the eyes till a blinded rooster bled into the sand.
My father ran where no one could see, spat up yesterday's rice and beans.

My grandfather's winnings paid for the rice and beans, the straw fedora,
the baseball glove in a box left behind by the Kings on the Día de Reyes.

A Brooklyn boy, I knew nothing of roosters, how the spurs of gamecocks
cut throats for sport, how a hammer strikes a cow between the eyes.
I was a big and hungry boy who only knew the taste of flesh was good.

OF THE THREADS THAT CONNECT THE STARS

for Klemente

Did you ever see stars? asked my father with a cackle. He was not
speaking of the heavens, but the white flash in his head when a fist burst
between his eyes. In Brooklyn, this would cause men and boys to slap
the table with glee; this might be the only heavenly light we'd ever see.

I never saw stars. The sky in Brooklyn was a tide of smoke rolling over us
from the factory across the avenue, the mattresses burning in the junkyard,
the ruins where squatters would sleep, the riots of 1966 that kept me
locked in my room like a suspect. My father talked truce on the streets.

My son can see the stars through the tall barrel of a telescope.
He names the galaxies with the numbers and letters of astronomy.
I cannot see what he sees in the telescope, no matter how many eyes I shut.
I understand a smoking mattress better than the language of galaxies.

My father saw stars. My son sees stars. The earth rolls beneath
our feet. We lurch ahead, and one day we have walked this far.

THE GODDAMNED CRUCIFIX

New York City, 1972

My father wandered through a dust storm in San Antonio
called diphtheria. By the time he stepped off the plane
in New York, his windpipe was closing. The doctors in the city
could not recognize a disease dead as polio, killed off
by vaccination years ago. In the emergency room, they said
Drink this, and my father almost drowned in a glass of water.

Now, many visitors came to pay homage on the ward
in the Catholic hospital, where the nurses and the crucifix
hovered over the bed. He did not want me there: *Don't let
him see me like this*, he said. I saw him: his black hair was white;
his brown skin was red; his ribs spread and his chest sank
with every rasping breath. He was skinny as a rubber chicken.

I leaned close to hear his last words, the dying wish I would
honor as his son for the rest of my life. And my father whispered:
Get that goddamned crucifix away from me. Honor thy father,
the Bible says, so I lifted Jesus off the nail on the wall
and hid Him in the drawer next to the bed, stuffed
back down into the darkness before the resurrection.
Only then did the miracle come to pass: my father lived.

EL MORIVIVÍ

In Memoriam
Frank Espada (1930–2014)

HAUNT ME

for my father

I am the archaeologist. I sift the shards of you: cufflinks, passport photos,
a button from the March on Washington with a black hand shaking
a white hand, letters in Spanish, your birth certificate from a town high
in the mountains. I cup your silence, and the silence melts like ice in a cup.

I search for you in two yellow Kodak boxes marked *Puerto Rico,*
Noche Buena, Diciembre 1968. In the 8-millimeter silence, the Espadas
gather, elders born before the Spanish-American War, my grandfather
on crutches after fracturing his fossil hip, his blind brother on a cane.
You greet the elders and they call you *Tato,* the name they call you there.
Uncles and cousins sing in a chorus of tongues without sound, vibration
of guitar strings stilled by an unseen hand, maracas shaking empty
of seeds. The camera wobbles from the singers to the television
and the astronauts sending pictures of the moon back to earth.
Down by the river, women still pound laundry on the rocks.

I am eleven again, a boy from the faraway city of ice that felled
my grandfather, startled after the blind man with the cane stroked
my face with his hand dry as straw, crying out *Bendito.* At the table,
I hear only the silence that rises like the river in my big ears.
You sit next to me, clowning for the camera, tugging the lapels
on your jacket, slicking back your black hair, brown skin darker
from days in the sun. You slide your arm around my shoulder,

your good right arm, your pitching arm, and my moon face radiates,
and the mountain song of my uncles and cousins plays in my head.

Watching you now, my face stings as it stung when my blind great-uncle
brushed my cheekbones, searching for his own face. When you died,
Tato, I took a razor to the movie looping in my head, cutting the scenes
where you curled an arm around my shoulder, all the times you would
squeeze the silence out of me so I could hear the cries and songs again.
When you died, I heard only the silences between us, the shouts belling
the air before the phone went dead, all the words melting like ice in a cup.
That way I could set my jaw and take my mother's hand at the mortuary,
greet the elders in my suit and tie at the memorial, say all the right words.

Yet, my face stings at last. I rewind and watch your arm drape across
my shoulder, over and over. A year ago, you pressed a Kodak slide
of my grandfather into my hand and said: *Next time, stay longer.*
Now, in the silence that is never silent, I push the chair away
from the table and say to you: *Sit down. Tell me everything. Haunt me.*

THE BEATING HEART OF THE WRISTWATCH

My father worked as a mechanic in the Air Force,
the engines of the planes howling in his ears all day.
One morning, the wristwatch his father gave him was gone.
The next day, he saw another soldier wearing the watch.
There was nothing he could say: no one would believe
the greaser airplane mechanic at the Air Force base
in San Antonio. Instead, one howling night he got drunk
and tore up the planks of an empty barracks for firewood.
There was no way for him to tell time locked in the brig.

When he died, I stole my father's wristwatch.
I listened to the beating heart of the watch.
The heart of the watch kept beating long after
my father's heart stopped beating. Somewhere,
the son of the man who stole my father's wristwatch
in the Air Force holds the watch to his ear and listens
to the heart of the watch beating. He keeps the watch
in a sacred place where no one else will hear it.
So the son tries to resurrect the father. The Bible
tells the story wrong. We try to resurrect the father.
We listen for the heartbeat and hear the howling.

ON THE HOVERING OF SOULS
AND BALLOON ANIMALS

for my father

We arrive at the Chapel by the Sea,
sign chipped away by winds off the Pacific.
As I steer my mother's hand from signature
to signature on the contracts and forms,
the woman at the mortuary, plump and rosy
as a balloon animal, files paperwork and chatters
on about the disposition of your *cremains*.

I want to rise, tear the check into fluttering gulls,
shout, *That's not a word*, and listen as my words
rattle like beads in the urn of her head. The urns
for sale circle us to eavesdrop on the negotiations.
I stifle a snort when she asks about your honorable
discharge from the Air Force, then offers us
an American flag, free to the families of veterans
with every white takeout box of *cremains*.

Before I can pour my glass of water on the contracts
and forms, my mother speaks: *He hated the Air Force.*
And he used to tell everyone he wasn't an American.
Then together, a mother-and-son vaudeville act,
we croon in chorus: *Can we get a Puerto Rican flag?*

The woman at the mortuary turns red and says,
Oh no. I wouldn't have any idea where to get one,
as if we demanded the flag planted on the moon
by the astronauts. I want to pop her with my pen
so she sails around the room like a balloon animal,
the way your soul would hover over my head
for eternity if I said *yes* to the flag of empire
folded in a triangle with your *cremains*, oh soul
of rebel flags shredded by hurricanes a world away.

BILLS TO PAY

for my mother

The night after my father died, I climbed the stairs
to tell my mother *goodnight.* I saw the left side of the bed
stacked with magazine clippings, newspapers, letters,
folders, unpaid bills, a Bible. *I slept with him for sixty-two years,*
she said. *I had to fill up his side of the bed.* I said the words
to her I should have said many times before. There were
words we still had time to say, and unpaid bills to pay.

AFTER THE GOOSE THAT ROSE
LIKE THE GOD OF GEESE

> *Everything that lives is Holy.*
> —*William Blake*

After the phone call about my father far away,
after the next-day flight canceled by the blizzard,
after the last words left unsaid between us,
after the harvest of the organs at the morgue,
after the mortuary and cremation of the body,
after the box of ashes shipped to my door by mail,
after the memorial service for him in Brooklyn,

I said: *I want to feed the birds. I want to feed bread*
to the birds. I want to feed bread to the birds at the park.

After the walk around the pond and the war memorial,
after the signs at every step that read, *Do Not Feed the Geese*,
after the goose that rose from the water like the god of geese,
after the goose that shrieked like a demon from the hell of geese,
after the goose that scattered the creatures smaller than geese,
after the hard beak, the wild mouth taking bread from my hand,

there was quiet in my head, no cacophony of the dead
lost in the catacombs, no mosquito hum of condolences,
only the next offering of bread raised up in my open hand,
the bread warm on the table of my truce with the world.

MAD LOVE

No one wants to look at pictures of Puerto Ricans, Frank.
—*Cornell Capa*

My brother said: *They harvested his corneas.* I imagined
the tweezers lifting the corneas from my father's eyes,
delicate as the wings of butterflies mounted under glass.
I imagined the transplant, stitches finer than hair,
eyes fluttering awake to the brilliance of an open window.

This is not a horror movie. This is not Peter Lorre in *Mad Love*,
the insane and jealous surgeon grafting the hands of a killer
onto the forearms of a concert pianist, who fumbles with the keys
of the piano, flings knives with lethal aim, *Moonlight Sonata*
swept away by lust for homicide, his wife shrieking.

The blind will see like the captain of the slave ship who turned the ship
around, voices in the room will praise the Lord for the miracle, yet
the eyes drinking light through my father's eyes will not see the faces
in the lens of his camera, faces of the faceless waking in the darkroom:

not the tomato picker with a picket sign on his shoulder that says
Reagan Steals from the Poor and Gives to the Rich; not the fry cook
in his fedora, staring at air as if he knew he would be stomped

to death on the stoop for an empty wallet; not the poet in a beret,
grinning at the vision of shoes for all the shoeless people on the earth;
not the dancer hearing the piano tell her to spin and spin again;
not the gravedigger and his machete, the bandanna that keeps the dust
of the dead from coating his tongue; not the union organizer, spirits
floating in the smoke of his victory cigar; not the addict in rehab gazing
at herself like a fortune-teller gazing at the cards; not the face half-hidden
by the star in the Puerto Rican flag, the darkness of his dissident's eye.

Now that my father cannot speak, they wait their turn to testify
in his defense, witnesses to the mad love that drove him to it.

SINKING OF THE *SAN JACINTO*

para mi padre

ng to this country was the worst thing
ever happened to me, you would say.
e steamship called the *San Jacinto*
ragged you from Puerto Rico to New York.
You swore in Spanish, dangling from the rails
like a nauseous acrobat, a seasick boy
who prayed to plunge over the side
and disappear into the green water.

A Nazi U-boat trailed behind the *San Jacinto*
on the voyage back to Puerto Rico. The torpedo
splintered the deck, six thousand tons creaking
and sinking into the sea. Among the dead:
Ramón Castillo, who shoveled the coal
into the furnace down below; Antonio Cortez,
who cleared the plates in the officers' mess,
daydreaming of La Parguera, the luminescent
bay, illumination of water on a moonless night.

You escaped the U-boat. Seven decades later,
the torpedo catches up to you, ripping through
your heart, and you sink into a moonless sea
like the six thousand tons of the *San Jacinto,*

Ramón Castillo and his shovelful of coal,
Antonio Cortez and his armload of plates.

I kissed the ground, you would say, sitting
at the kitchen table in Brooklyn, and I tried
to imagine licking the dirt off my own lips.
Years after the *San Jacinto* took you away,
you would return to your island, step off
the plane, drop to your knees at the airport
and kiss the ground. Back you came to Brooklyn,
a car stalled on the highway, steam pouring
from the hood, when all you wanted
was the sand of the beach burning your feet.

Now, if your ancestors wait for you anywhere,
they wait on the shores of the bay at La Parguera.
May you navigate through the night without
the compass devoured by the salt of the sea.
May you rise up in the luminescent bay,
stirring the microscopic creatures in the water
back to life so their light startles your eyes.
May the water glow blue as a hyacinth in your hands.

THERE BUT NOT THERE

the way they look at you.
you don't know if it's something you did
or something you are.
—Tino Villanueva

I was my father's catcher at Highland Park in Brooklyn,
bracing myself for the curveball that started to spin
at my left shoulder and bounced off my right knee,
as I swatted with my yawning mitt and missed it.
He would roar at my bulging eyes, the stupefaction
of a boy studying a magician's every move, unable
to figure out the trick. I squeezed the fingers of his glove,
wrinkled and black, like shaking hands with a gorilla.

During the War, my father taught himself the grips,
the spins, the drops, the in-shoots, the knuckleball
to pitch for the team paid for by the Democratic Party
ward boss of the Upper West Side, who counted out
the cash for the uniforms and the team bus, put up
the stakes on every game, collected on the bets.

The skinny refugee from Puerto Rico pitched every game,
even the game at the pig farm in the land of Weehawken.
New Jersey was wild in those days, he said. *We played in pig shit.*
Somebody gored the second baseman on the slide, punches

fell like hail from a clear sky, and the pig farmers chased
the team back to the bus, the driver in a whiskey haze
as he spun the wheel, tires spitting mud at the mob.

Once, my father told me of the day his curveball was a cloud
of steam, a spirit there but not there, a hummingbird
blurring in the eyes of the hitters, dipping away from the bat,
the day he no-hit the American Legion team from Queens,
the day he turned fifteen and would live forever.

The big-league scouts watched him pitch at Central Park.
I didn't throw hard enough for them, he said. *Or maybe
it was my dark skin. They loved blond hair and blue eyes.*
He never knew, and so the scouts would visit him in sleep,
notching illegible notes on a clipboard, there but not there.

There is a browning photograph of my father in his uniform
from 1947, tilting into his windup, spikes high to dazzle
the batter, knuckles almost scraping the grass behind him,
ready to fire the spin, the drop, the curveball. There is no baseball
in his hand. The magician in him made the baseball disappear.
His pitching hand rolls into a fist for all the scouts to see.

Eddie McClain from 108th Street, my father's catcher seventy years ago,
the best man at his wedding, shook my hand at the memorial service
in Brooklyn. Sweating in my suit and tie, I never had a chance
to ask him for the secret, how he caught the curveball, that cloud
of steam, the flight of the hummingbird, my father there but not there.

THE SHAMROCK

My father was a Shamrock, not the kind blooming everywhere
on Saint Patrick's Day, but a Puerto Rican Shamrock, wearing
the white clover emblazoned on green trunks, loping down court
with the Maloney twins, Fitzgerald and Plunkett. My father
was brown as an Indian Head penny, the center on the team,
flipping his hook at the backboard, shoving two-handed set shots
from the chest, elbows sharp wings on the rebound beneath
the basket at PS 165 on West 108th Street. Another boy yelled
Hey, Pancho and slapped him off the brick wall behind the basket.
Pancho swung as he bounced off the wall, bursting the boy's nose
like a hydrant of blood, spraying red on a summer night in the city.

My father was a Shamrock all his life. He hammered up the backboard
and the basket in the driveway for me to practice free throws, the only
Puerto Rican at Central High in Valley Stream. I listened to the echo
of the ball on concrete, the clatter off the rim. The day a boy yelled
Foul, you spic, I swung and scraped my knuckles on his belt buckle,
too far away to stain his teeth with blood. I set picks, standing still
as defenders rammed blindly into me. My father was a Shamrock,
and so was Anaya, the other Pancho from West 108th Street,
the day the three of us took the court against the unknown men
who swaggered up the driveway, who hooted at the two-handed
set shots, the ball sailing from another century, till it plopped
through the net. The Shamrocks flipped the ball behind the back,

twirling layups in the air as I set picks, speared by the shoulders
of the invaders. We won, and my fingers traced the bruises on my chest.

My father was a Puerto Rican Shamrock, the only atheist in a Catholic
neighborhood, debating the miracles of the saints with the baffled
Irish boys on the team. Now, his ashes sit in a white box on a chair
by my desk, an altar without saints or candles or holy cards. Atop
the box there is a snapshot of the Shamrocks, the Maloney twins,
Fitzgerald, Anaya and Espada, in suits and ties for Christmas dinner
on West 108th Street. When I had to sign for the box at the doorstep,
ball-handler that I am, I dropped it. I ask for forgiveness at the altar.
In the photograph, my father kneels. His hand spreads to grip the grain
of a basketball on the floor. He is the center of the team. He is seventeen.

EL MORIVIVÍ

In Memoriam Frank Espada (1930–2014)

The Spanish means: *I died, I lived.* In Puerto Rico, the leaves
of el morivivi close in the dark and open at first light.
The fronds curl at a finger's touch and then unfurl again.
My father, a mountain born of mountains, the tallest
Puerto Rican in New York, who scraped doorways,
who could crack the walls with the rumble of his voice,
kept a morivivi growing in his ribs. He would die, then live.

My father spoke in the tongue of el morivivi, teaching me
the parable of Joe Fleming, who screwed his lit cigarette
into the arms of the spics he caught, flapping like fish.
My father was a bony boy, the nerves in his back
crushed by the Aiello Coal and Ice Company, the load
he lifted up too many flights of stairs. Three times
they would meet to brawl for a crowd after school.
The first time, my father opened his eyes to gravel
and the shoes of his enemy. The second time, he rose
and dug his arm up to the elbow in the monster's belly,
so badly did he want to tear out the heart and eat it.
The third time, Fleming did not show up, and the boys
with cigarette burns clapped their spindly champion
on the back, all the way down the street. Fleming would

become a cop, fired for breaking bones in too many faces.
He died smoking in bed, a sheet of flame up to his chin.

There was a moriv003 sprouting in my father's chest. He would die,
then live. He spat obscenities like sunflower seeds at the driver
who told him to sit at the back of the bus in Mississippi, then
slipped his cap over his eyes and fell asleep. He spent a week in jail,
called it the best week of his life, strode through the jailhouse door
and sat behind the driver of the bus on the way out of town,
his Air Force uniform all that kept the noose from his neck.
He would come to know the jailhouse again, among hundreds
of demonstrators ferried by police to Hart Island on the East River,
where the City of New York stacks the coffins of anonymous
and stillborn bodies. Here, Confederate prisoners once wept
for the Stars and Bars; now, the prisoners sang Freedom Songs.
The jailers outlawed phone calls, so we were sure my father must be
a body like the bodies rolling waterlogged in the East River, till he came
back from the island of the dead, black hair combed meticulously.
When the riots burned in Brooklyn night after night, my father
was a peacemaker on the corner with a megaphone. A fiery
chunk of concrete fell from the sky and missed his head by inches.
My mother would tell me: *Your father is out dodging bullets.*
He spoke at a rally with Malcolm X, incantatory words
billowing through the bundled crowd, lifting hands and faces.
Teach, they cried. My father clicked a photograph of Malcolm
as he bent to hear a question, finger pressed against the chin.
Two months later, the assassins stampeded the crowd

to shoot Malcolm, blood leaping from his chest as he fell.
My father would die too, but then he would live again,
after every riot, every rally, every arrest, every night in jail,
the change from his pockets landing hard on the dresser
at 4 AM every time I swore he was gone for good.

My father knew the secrets of el morivíví, that he would die,
then live. He drifted off at the wheel, drove into a guardrail,
shook his head and walked away without a web of scars
or fractures. He passed out from the heat in the subway,
toppled onto the tracks and somehow missed the third rail.
He tied a white apron across his waist to open a grocery store,
pulled a revolver from the counter to startle the gangsters
demanding protection, then put up signs for a clearance sale
as soon as they backed out the door with their hands in the air.
When the family finally took a vacation in the mountains
of the Hudson Valley, a hotel with waiters in white jackets
and white paint peeling in the room, the roof exploded
in flame, as if the ghost of Joe Fleming and his cigarette
trailed us everywhere, and it was then that my father
appeared in the smoke, like a general leading the charge
in battle, shouting commands at the volunteer fire company,
steering the water from the hoses, since he was immune
to death by fire or water, as if he wore the crumbled leaves
of el morivíví in an amulet slung around his neck.

My brother called to say el morivíví was gone. My father tore
at the wires, the electrodes, the IV, saying that he wanted

to go home. The hospital was a jailhouse in Mississippi.
The furious pulse that fired his heart in every fight flooded
the chambers of his heart. The doctors scrutinized the film,
the grainy shadows and the light, but could never see: my father
was a morivíví. *I died. I lived.* He died. He lived. He dies. He lives.

Notes on the Poems

Vivas to Those Who Have Failed: The Paterson Silk Strike, 1913: "Vivas to those who have fail'd! . . ." The title of this sonnet cycle and the epigraph by Walt Whitman come from section 18 of "Song of Myself." The Paterson Silk Strike (February–July 1913) was one of the most significant strikes in United States history. Led by labor organizers from the Industrial Workers of the World (IWW), more than twenty-five thousand mostly immigrant workers walked out, shutting down three hundred mills in Paterson, New Jersey. Over three thousand people were arrested. The strike was defeated, but the key demand—for an eight-hour day—would transform American labor.

The Red Flag: "The red flag of anarchy . . ." The first stanza quotes "To the City Authorities, the Silk Manufacturers, and the Forces of Law and Order in Paterson," an editorial in the *Paterson Daily Press*, March 10, 1913. The first stanza also derives in part from "The Rip in the Silk Industry" by William D. "Big Bill" Haywood in the *International Socialist Review*, May 1913. Haywood was a major figure in the labor movement, a cofounder and leader of the IWW.

The River Floods the Avenue: On April 17, 1913, Joseph Cutherton of the O'Brien Detective Agency, hired by the Weidmann Silk Dyeing Company, shot and killed bystander Modestino Valentino in the presence of numerous witnesses. He was never indicted. The second stanza quotes Carlo Tresca's "blood for blood" eulogy. Tresca was an Italian anarchist, editor, orator, labor organizer and leader of the IWW. The first stanza relies in part on "Modestino Valentino Remembered, 100 Years Later" in the *Paterson Times*, April 22, 2013, and *The Fragile Bridge: Paterson Silk Strike, 1913* (Temple University Press, 1988) by Steve Golin. The second stanza relies in part on *Carlo Tresca: Portrait of a Rebel* (AK Press, 2010) by Nunzio Pernicone.

The Insects in the Soup: "There's war in Paterson . . ." The second stanza quotes—and the poem relies upon—"War in Paterson" by John Reed in *The Masses*, June 1913. Reed was a major journalist who was radicalized by his experience of the Paterson strike. He soon accompanied Pancho Villa, the Commander of the División del Norte during the Mexican Revolution, and wrote an account of the Revolution called *Insurgent Mexico* (D. Appleton and Company, 1914). The subject of the film *Reds*, Reed is best known for his account of the Bolshevik Revolution, *Ten Days That Shook the World* (Boni and Liveright, 1919).

The Little Agitator: Elizabeth Gurley Flynn dubbed Hannah Silverman "The Joan of Arc of the Silk Strike." The first stanza derives in part from "Paterson Strikers Mild" in *The New York Times*, June 21, 1913; the poem also relies on *The Fragile Bridge: Paterson Silk Strike, 1913* by Steve Golin.

Vivas to Those Who Have Failed: This poem is based in part on an email correspondence with poet and professor Maria Mazziotti Gillan in December 2013. "Mazziotti" refers to Arturo Mazziotti, the father of Maria, who was a labor organizer in the 1930s. The "Sons of Italy" refers to a fraternal organization instrumental in uniting the Italian community in Paterson behind the strike; the "Workmen's Circle" refers to a fraternal organization that performed the same function in the Jewish community. "Local 152" refers to the affiliate of the IWW that played a key role in initiating the strike. "One-eyed Big Bill" refers to the fact that Bill Haywood was blind in his right eye. "Flynn the Rebel Girl" refers to Elizabeth Gurley Flynn, a socialist, orator and leader of the IWW, beloved by the strikers. Joe Hill wrote his song "The Rebel Girl" in honor of Flynn.

The Right Foot of Juan de Oñate: Don Juan de Oñate y Salazar was a Spanish conquistador who founded Santa Fé de Nuevo México and became the first governor. In January 1599, Oñate suppressed the resistance of the Acoma Pueblo by killing eight hundred villagers and enslaving five hundred more. By Oñate's order, Spanish troops amputated the right foot of all Acoma men over the age of twenty-five. In 1998, a Native American group used an electric saw to cut off the right foot of the statue at the Oñate Monument and Visitors Center in Alcalde, New Mexico. In 2007, another statue of Oñate—the largest equestrian statue in the world—was installed at El Paso International Airport. The poem is based on visits to the sites in Alcalde and El Paso, in the company of novelist John Nichols and scholar Arturo Madrid, respectively, and on conversations with both. Background sources include *Lies Across America: What Our Historic Sites Get Wrong* (New Press, 1999) by James Loewen; "Oñate's Right Foot" by Margaret Randall in *Liberation Lit*, March 31, 2008; and "Conquistador Statue Stirs Hispanic Pride and Indian Rage" by James Brooke in *The New York Times*, September 23, 2009.

Heal the Cracks in the Bell of the World: On December 14, 2012, gunman Adam Lanza killed twenty students—ages six to seven—and six educators at the Sandy Hook Elementary School in Newtown, Connecticut. This poem is based on a visit to Newtown, and was written for the occasion of a National Children's Day event entitled "Within Our Reach" at the Newtown Congregational Church on June 8, 2013. The "city where children gathered copper shells" is Tirana, Albania, site of the "Bell of Peace;" "I was born of bullets" comes from the bell's inscription. The city "where cannons from the armies of the Great War / sank into molten metal" is Roverto, Italy, site of the "Campana dei Caduti (Bell of the Fallen)" or "Maria Dolens" bell.

How We Could Have Lived or Died This Way: "Not songs of loyalty alone are these..." The epigraph comes from "To a Foil'd European Revolutionaire" by Walt Whitman. "The immigrant street vendor" refers to Amadou Diallo, an unarmed twenty-two-year-old immigrant from Guinea shot nineteen times and killed by four New York City police officers in the Bronx on February 4, 1999. "The deaf woodcarver" refers to John T. Williams, a fifty-year-old Native American artisan shot and killed by a police officer in Seattle, Washington on August 30, 2010. "The minister's heart" refers to Accelyne Williams, a seventy-five-year-old Methodist minister from Antigua who had a heart attack and died in police custody after a mistaken drug raid on his apartment in the Dorchester community of Boston, Massachusetts on March 25, 1994. "The man hawking / a fistful of cigarettes" refers to Eric Garner, an unarmed forty-three-year-old African-American and asthmatic who died after a chokehold applied by a New York City police officer on Staten Island on July 17, 2014. "The conga player" refers to Martín "Tito" Pérez, a thirty-one-year-old Puerto Rican musician and photographer who died in police custody—alleged to have hanged himself with his hands cuffed behind him—in the East Harlem community of New York City on December 1, 1974. "The suspect / leaking blood from his chest" refers to Victor White III, a twenty-two-year-old African-American who died in police custody—said to have shot himself while handcuffed in the backseat of a squad car—in Iberia Parish, Louisiana on March 3, 2014. "The 300-pound boy" and "the body left in the street" refer to Michael Brown, an unarmed eighteen-year-old African-American shot six times and killed by a police officer in Ferguson, Missouri on August 9, 2014. "The next Black man, fleeing" refers to Walter Scott, an unarmed fifty-year-old African-American shot five times and killed by a police officer in North Charleston, South Carolina on April 4, 2015. "The rebels marching, hands upraised" refers to the protests in Ferguson, Missouri and elsewhere after the Michael Brown killing.

Chalkboard on the Wall of a Diner in Providence, Rhode Island the Morning After George Zimmerman Was Acquitted in the Shooting Death of Trayvon Martin, an Unarmed Black Teenager: Trayvon Martin, an unarmed seventeen-year-old African-American, was shot to death by neighborhood watch volunteer George Zimmerman in Sanford, Florida on February 26, 2012. Zimmerman was acquitted of second-degree murder and manslaughter charges in July 2013, provoking national outrage. The poem quotes "Letter from a Birmingham Jail" by Martin Luther King Jr.

Ghazal for a Tall Boy from New Hampshire: James Foley (1973–2014) was born in Evanston, Illinois and grew up in Wolfeboro, New Hampshire. He received his Master of Fine Arts degree in fiction from the University of Massachusetts in 2003. (I served on his thesis commitee.) From 2002 to 2004, he taught English to Spanish speakers at The Care Center, a High School Equivalency and alternative education program for adolescent mothers in Holyoke, Massachusetts. Foley obtained a journalism degree and ultimately became a freelance war correspondent, working for *GlobalPost* and *Agence France-Presse*. While reporting on the Syrian Civil War, he was abducted in November 2012. ISIS (the Islamic State of Iraq and al-Sham) executed James Foley by beheading in Al-Raqqah, Syria on August 19, 2014.

Here I Am: The son of Portuguese immigrants, José "JoeGo" Gouveia was a poet, journalist, organizer and radio personality. He served as Poet in Residence at Cape Cod Community College and Poetry Curator at the Cultural Center of Cape Cod. He wrote the "Meter Man" poetry column for *The Barnstable Patriot* in Hyannis and hosted the "Poets' Corner" radio show on WOMR-FM in Provincetown, Massachusetts. He published one full-length collection of poems, *Saudades*, with Casa Mariposa Press. At Gouveia's request, this poem was included in his book as the foreword. He died in May 2014 at age forty-nine, one month after the book was published.

Barbaric Yawp Big Noise Blues: "I. Celebrate. Myself . . ." Stanza four quotes sections 1, 33 and 52 from "Song of Myself" by Walt Whitman. David Lenson is a veteran saxophone player who has worked with blues musicians John Lee Hooker, Muddy Waters and Buddy Guy, as well as his own group, the Reprobate Blues Band. He is also a retired professor of Comparative Literature at the University of Massachusetts–Amherst. This poem is based on a visit with Lenson at a Northampton, Massachusetts nursing home in September 2013.

Castles for the Laborers and Ballgames on the Radio: Howard Zinn was a major historian, teacher and political activist. His landmark work, *A People's History of the United States* (Harper & Row, 1980), has sold more than two million copies. Sandy Koufax was a Hall of Fame pitcher for the Brooklyn/Los Angeles Dodgers. This poem is based on a visit to Zinn's house in Auburndale, Massachusetts in January 2009.

From the *Rubáiyát of Fenway Park*: The poem is a parody of verse 51 of the *Rubáiyát of Omar Khayyám* as translated by Edward FitzGerald: "The Moving Finger writes; and, having writ, / Moves on: nor all thy Piety nor Wit / Shall lure it back to cancel half a Line, / Nor all thy Tears wash out a Word of it."

Marshmallow Rice Krispie Treat Machu Picchu: "All the world's a stage . . ." This is the first line from the famed monologue called "The Seven Ages of Man," spoken by Jaques in Act II, Scene vii of Shakespeare's *As You Like It*. The poem quotes the monologue in stanzas one, four and six. Anthony Quinn played an aging boxer in the film *Requiem for a Heavyweight* (1962). "Machu Picchu" refers to the site of fifteenth-century Inca ruins in the Andean highlands of Perú, made famous by an epic poem, *Alturas de Macchu Picchu (The Heights of Macchu Picchu)* by Pablo Neruda. Francisco Pizarro González was the Spanish conquistador who conquered the Inca Empire in 1533. The "DVD of *The Crucible*" refers to the 1996 film version of the Arthur Miller play based on the Salem witch trials.

Flowers and Bullets: "Cuba and Puerto Rico . . ." The epigraph comes from "Cuba y Puerto Rico Son" by Lola Rodríguez de Tió, a Puerto Rican poet and advocate of independence for both islands. José Martí was a major Cuban poet, essayist, translator, journalist and leader of the Cuban independence movement. After years of exile, he returned to Cuba in 1895, where he was killed by Spanish troops at the Battle of Dos Ríos.

A Million Ants Swarming Through His Body: José Luis "Chegüí" Torres, from Playa Ponce, Puerto Rico, was light-heavyweight boxing champion of the world (1965–66). He won the title with a ninth-round knockout of Willie Pastrano at Madison Square Garden in March 1966. He retired following his second-round knockout of Charlie "Devil" Green at Madison Square Garden in July 1969, after being knocked down in the first round. Inducted into the International Boxing Hall of Fame in 1997, Torres became a writer, mentored by Norman Mailer and Pete Hamill. He published two books—*Sting Like a Bee: The Muhammad Ali Story* (Abelard-Schuman, 1971) and *Fire and Fear: The Inside Story of Mike Tyson* (Warner Books, 1989)—and wrote columns in English and Spanish for various New York newspapers. The poem is based on personal conversations with Torres. In conversation and in *Sting Like a Bee*, he compared the experience of being knocked down to the sensation of "a million ants" entering the body, thus providing the title for the poem. The third stanza derives in part from an Associated Press report of the Pastrano bout in the *Chicago Tribune*, March 31, 1966. The fourth stanza relies on a quote from Pete Hamill in "Torres' Legacy Extends Beyond the Ropes" by George Kimball on ESPN.com, January 20, 2009.

The Discovery of Archaeopteryx: *Archaeopteryx* was a transitional form between birds and dinosaurs. The poem is based on a visit to Puerto Rico in December 1968. "Gallos de pelea" means "gamecocks." "Día de Reyes" refers to Three Kings' Day, the Epiphany as celebrated throughout Latin America.

Of the Threads That Connect the Stars: The title comes from section 24 of "Song of Myself" by Walt Whitman.

Haunt Me: "Noche Buena" refers to Christmas Eve. "Bendito," which literally means "blessed," is a common Puerto Rican expression, used here as a term of affection. In the second stanza, "the Spanish-American War" refers to the invasion and colonization of Puerto Rico by the United States in 1898. "The astronauts sending pictures of the moon" refers to Apollo 8.

After the Goose That Rose Like the God of Geese: "Everything that lives is Holy . . ." The epigraph comes from *The Marriage of Heaven and Hell* by William Blake.

Mad Love: "No one wants to look at pictures of Puerto Ricans, Frank . . ." The epigraph comes from a personal conversation between Frank Espada and noted photographer Cornell Capa. My father would go on to found and direct the Puerto Rican Diaspora Documentary Project, a photo-documentary and oral history of the Puerto Rican migration, resulting in more than forty solo exhibitions and the publication of a book entitled *The Puerto Rican Diaspora: Themes in the Survival of a People* in 2006. His photographs are included in the collections of the Smithsonian Institution and the Library of Congress. The title and second stanza refer to the classic horror film *Mad Love* (1935). In the third stanza, "the captain of the slave ship" refers to Captain John Newton, the former slaver who wrote the hymn "Amazing Grace." The fourth stanza refers to a series of photographs from the Puerto Rican Diaspora Documentary Project.

"The fry cook / in his fedora" refers to a photograph of Agropino Bonillo, murdered in East New York, Brooklyn in 1966. "The poet in a beret / grinning at the vision of shoes for all the shoeless people on the earth" refers to a photograph of Jack Agüeros and his poem "Psalm for Distribution." The "gravedigger and his machete" refers to a photograph of Jaime Jenkins in Utuado, Puerto Rico, my father's birthplace. The "union organizer" refers to a photograph of Edelmiro Huertas, who organized San Francisco's furniture factories in the 1930s.

The Sinking of the *San Jacinto*: According to multiple sources, a Nazi U-boat torpedoed and sank the steamship *San Jacinto*, en route from New York to Puerto Rico, on April 22, 1942. Listed among the fourteen dead were Ramón Castillo, a fireman, and Antonio Cortez, a messman. La Parguera is a bioluminescent bay on the southwest coast of Puerto Rico, inhabited by microscopic dinoflagellates that glow when the water is disturbed. "Jacinto" means "hyacinth."

There But Not There: "the way they look at you . . ." The epigraph comes from the poem "Not Knowing, in Aztlán" by Tino Villanueva.

El Morivivi: "Morivivi" ("I died/I lived") is the term, in Puerto Rican Spanish, for the pantropical weed classified as *Mimosa pudica*. *Pudica* is the Latin for "bashful" or "shrinking," a reference to the plant's shrinking reaction to contact. The second stanza derives from an unpublished essay by my father called "The Beast." The third stanza describes my father's history of political activism, beginning in December 1949, when he was arrested and jailed in Biloxi, Mississippi for refusing to sit at the back of the bus. In April 1964, he was arrested and jailed again along with three hundred other protesters associated with the Brooklyn chapter of CORE (the Congress of Racial Equality) for demonstrating at the New York World's Fair. The protesters were locked up incommunicado at a jail on Hart Island in the East River, the site of a Confederate prisoner-of-war camp in 1865 and still the potter's field for the city of New York, where almost one million people have been buried since 1869. (This passage relies in part on "Visiting the Island of the Dead" by Corey Kilgannon in *The New York Times*, November 15, 2013.) As the head of a community organization called East New York Action, my father was called in to act as peacemaker during the riots in the community. In December 1964, he spoke at a rally in Brooklyn for community control of schools with Malcolm X. He photographed Malcolm taking questions after the rally; it is his most celebrated photograph. Malcolm X was assassinated in February 1965. This poem was written for the occasion of my father's memorial at El Puente, a community center in Williamsburg, Brooklyn, on May 17, 2014.

About Martín Espada

Called by Sandra Cisneros "the Pablo Neruda of North American authors," Martín Espada was born in Brooklyn, New York in 1957. He has published more than fifteen books as a poet, editor, essayist and translator. His collections of poems include *The Trouble Ball* (2011), *The Republic of Poetry* (2006), *Alabanza* (2003), *A Mayan Astronomer in Hell's Kitchen* (2000), *Imagine the Angels of Bread* (1996) and *City of Coughing and Dead Radiators* (1993). His many honors include the Shelley Memorial Award, the Robert Creeley Award, the National Hispanic Cultural Center Literary Award, an American Book Award, the PEN/Revson Fellowship and a Guggenheim Fellowship. *The Republic of Poetry* was a finalist for the Pulitzer Prize. The title poem of his collection *Alabanza*, about 9/11, has been widely anthologized and performed. His book of essays, *Zapata's Disciple* (1998), was banned in Tucson as part of the Mexican-American Studies Program outlawed by the state of Arizona. A graduate of Northeastern University Law School and a former tenant lawyer in Greater Boston's Latino community, Espada is a professor of English at the University of Massachusetts–Amherst.